THE ULTIMATE SASKATOON BERRY COOKBOOK

VICKIANNE CASWELL

PUBLISHED BY

4Paws
Games and
Publishing

BRUNO, SASKATCHEWAN, CANADA

The Ultimate Saskatoon Berry Cookbook

Written by Vickianne Caswell

Cover Art by 4 Paws Games and Publishing

Edited by 4 Paws Games and Publishing

Text Areas by 4 Paws Games and Publishing

Formatted and Published by 4 Paws Games and Publishing

First publication

Published December 2017

ISBN-13: 978-1-988345-57-4

ISBN-10: 198834557X

Published by 4 Paws Games and Publishing

P.O. Box 444

Humboldt, Saskatchewan, Canada S0K 2A0

http://www.4-Paws-Games-and-Publishing.ca

Find Vickianne, Freckles and Sherlock Online

Website

http://vickianne-caswell.weebly.com/

http://www.freckles-the-bunny-series.ca/

http://www.sherlock-the-remarkable-cat-series.ca/

Facebook

https://www.facebook.com/Vickianne.Caswell.Author

https://www.facebook.com/Freckles.The.Bunny.Series

https://www.facebook.com/SherlockTheRemarkableCatSeries

https://www.facebook.com/The-Adventures-of-Tipsy-Tail-514438432252826

Amazon Authors Central Page

https://www.amazon.com/Vickianne-Caswell/e/B00D1RL73I/

Buy Signed Copies

http://www.4-paws-games-and-publishing.ca/store.html

Other Books by Vickianne Caswell

FRECKLES THE BUNNY SERIES

TRUE TAILS OF FRECKLES AND HER FRIENDS (A FRECKLES THE BUNNY SERIES COMPANION BOOK)

1: FRECKLES IS SCARED OF SCHOOL

2: FRECKLES AND THE LESS FORTUNATE

3: FRECKLES LENDS A PAW

4: FRECKLES AND THE TRUE MEANING OF CHRISTMAS

5: FRECKLES AND THE COST OF POPULARITY

6: THE FRECKLE MONSTER

SHERLOCK THE REMARKABLE CAT SERIES

1: SHERLOCK, THE CAT WHO COULDN'T MEOW

THE ADVENTURES OF TIPSY TAIL

Coming 2018.

THE ULTIMATE COOKBOOKS

THE ULTIMATE CHERRY COOKBOOK

THE ULTIMATE SASKATOON BERRY COOKBOOK

THE ULTIMATE BLUEBERRY COOKBOOK (coming 2018)

THE ULTIMATE MAPLE COOKBOOK (coming 2018)

THE ULTIMATE PUMPKIN COOKBOOK (coming 2018)

Table of Contents

Saskatoon Berries and You

Per 100 grams serving:

Calories: 85 calories

Protein: 1.3 grams

Carbohydrates: 18.5 grams

Calcium: 88 milligrams

Fiber: 5.93 grams

Vitamin C: 3.55 milligrams

Iron: 0.96 milligrams

Potassium: 162 milligrams

Vitamin A: 35.68 IU

Saskatoon Berries are 11% of the recommended daily intake of calcium. [1]

---

[1] http://www.bylands.com/blog-entry/health-benefits-saskatoon-berries

6 Interesting Facts

1. Were consumed by the Indigenous Aboriginals of Canada for their nutritional & medicinal benefits.

2. Are native to North America.

3. Have 2 times more Fiber, Potassium & Iron than blueberries.

4. Have 4 times more Magnesium than Blueberries.

5. Naturally rich dark royal purple colour comes from anthocyanins. [2]

6. Are sometimes called Serviceberries.

Freezing Saskatoon Berries

Rinse them in a colander and drain well. Lay on single layers of parchment paper (works best on a cookie sheet) and place in the freezer. Freeze until solid. Once solid, place into a Ziploc® freezer bag.

---

[2] https://prairieberries.com/health-nutrition/

Alcohol Drinks

Saskatoon Sour

Ingredients

1 Ounce Pisco

1/2 Ounce Saskatoon liqueur

1/2 Ounce lime juice

1/2 Ounce simple syrup

1 Egg white

Saskatoon berry garnish

Directions

Combine all ingredients except garnish in a cocktail shaker and dry shake to emulsify the egg. Add ice and shake again. Strain into a coupe or rocks glass and garnish with a Saskatoon berry.

Saskatoon Berry Buck

Ingredients

1-1/2 Ounce Canadian whisky

1/2 Ounce fresh lime juice

2 Teaspoons Saskatoon berry jam

3 Ounces ginger ale

Lime wheel for garnish

Directions

To a cocktail shaker filled with ice, add whisky, lime juice and jam. Shake for 20 seconds and then double strain into a highball filled with ice. Top with ginger ale. Garnish with lime wheel.

The Saskatoon

Ingredients

1-1/2 Ounce Canadian rye whisky®

1/2 Ounce dry vermouth

1/2 Ounce Saskatoon berry liqueur®

1/2 Ounce Cynar®

Bar spoon of Fernet-Branca®

2 Dashes of rhubarb bitters

Directions

In an ice-filled mixing glass, add all ingredients and stir for 30 seconds, until chilled and diluted. Strain into a chilled coupe glass. Garnish with a Saskatoon berry.

Saskatoon Wine Recipe 1

Ingredients

3-4 Pounds Saskatoon berries

2 Pounds granulated sugar

2 Juiced lemons

1 Teaspoon pectic enzyme

5 Pints water

1 Crushed Campden tablet

Wine yeast and nutrient

Directions

Pick only ripe berries. Wash, destem and crush berries. Put in primary with sugar, lemon juice, water, and crushed Campden tablet, stirring well to dissolve sugar. Cover with muslin and put in a warm place. Add pectic enzyme after 12 hours and wine yeast and nutrient after additional 12 hours. Stir twice daily for 5 days. Strain through a medium-meshed nylon sieve, pressing lightly to extract juice, returning liquor to the primary. Recover primary and wait 24 hours, then syphon off sediment into the secondary and fit airlock, adjusting the volume to allow 3 inches of space for foaming. Move to a cooler place. When vigorous fermentation subsides (10 to 14 days), top up with water or reserved juice. Ferment additional 2 weeks, then rack into clean secondary. Refit airlock and rack after 30 days. Wait another 30 days, rack again and bottle. This is a very good dry wine, fit to taste after 6 months. Improves with additional ageing.

‡ Two gallons of berries should make 5 gallons of wine.

Saskatoon wine Recipe 2

Ingredients

2-3 Pounds Saskatoon berries

2-1/2 Pounds granulated sugar

2 Juiced lemons

1 Teaspoon pectic enzyme

5-7 Pints water

Wine yeast and nutrient

Directions

Pick only ripe berries. Wash, destem and crush berries. Heat to low boil, reduce heat and simmer covered for 10 minutes. Fold top berries under, recover and simmer another 10 minutes. Pour into nylon jelly-bag and allow to drip over primary until pulp is cool. Meanwhile, dissolve sugar into 3 cups boiling water and allow to cool. Add juice, jelly-bag, juice of 2 lemons, yeast nutrients, and pectic enzyme to the primary. Wait at least 10 hours before inoculating with wine yeast. Cover well and set in warm (70 to 75°F) place, stirring twice daily. When S.G. drops to 1.040 (about 5 days), gently press jelly-bag to extract clear juice, discarding remaining pulp and seed. Siphon off sediments into secondary, top up, fit airlock, and set in cooler (60 to 65°F) place. Rack after 30 days and again after another 30 days. Bottle when clear, racking only if additional sediments have formed. Store in dark place to preserve deep ruby colour. May taste after 6 months but improves with age.

‡ One and one-half gallons of berries should make 5 gallons of wine.

Saskatoon Wine Recipe 3

Ingredients

2-3 Pounds Saskatoon berries

1 Pounds raisins

2-1/2 Pounds granulated sugar

1 Teaspoon pectic enzyme

5-7 Pints water

Wine yeast and nutrient

Directions

Pick only ripe berries. Wash, destem and crush berries. Heat to low boil, reduce heat and simmer covered for 10 minutes. Fold top berries under, recover and simmer another 10 minutes. Pour into nylon jelly-bag and allow to drip over primary until pulp is cool. Meanwhile, dissolve sugar into 3 cups boiling water and allow to cool. Chop or mince raisins and put in second jelly-bag. Add juice, both jelly-bags, all but 2/3 cup sugar-water, pectic enzyme, and yeast nutrients to the primary. Wait at least 10 hours before inoculating with wine yeast. Cover well and set in warm (70 to 75°F) place, stirring twice daily. After 5 days, gently press jelly-bag of Saskatoon to extract clear juice, discarding remaining pulp and seed. Recover and ferment additional five days. Gently squeeze raisin jelly-bag to extract juice, then discard pulp. Siphon off sediments into secondary, add remaining sugar-water, top up, fit airlock, and set in cooler (60 to 65°F) place. Rack three times at 30-day intervals. Bottle when clear, racking again only if additional sediments have formed. Store in dark place to preserve deep ruby colour. May taste after 9 months but improves with age.

‡ This is a full-bodied wine.

Breads

Saskatoon Berry Banana Bread

Ingredients

2 Large eggs, room temperature

1 Cup brown sugar

1/3 Cup vegetable oil

1-1/4 Cup mashed banana (2-3 *very* ripe bananas)

1-1/2 Teaspoons vanilla extract

3/4 Teaspoon almond extract

2-2/3 Cup all-purpose flour

1 Teaspoon baking soda

1 Teaspoon baking powder

1 Teaspoon salt

1-1/2 Teaspoon cinnamon

1/2 Teaspoon nutmeg

1 Cup yoghurt – strawberry (or another berry) flavoured

1/2 to 3/4 Cup fresh or frozen Saskatoon berries, in small pieces

Directions

Preheat the oven to 350°F.

In a medium-sized bowl, beat together the eggs, sugar, and oil. Blend in the mashed banana, vanilla, and almond extract. Stir in the cinnamon and nutmeg. Whisk together.

In a small mixing bowl, sift the flour, baking soda, baking powder, and salt. Add to the banana mixture. Mix gently but thoroughly, then fold in the yoghurt, just until combined. Fold in the berries.

Pour the batter into a well-greased 9×5-inch loaf pan. Bake the bread for about 55 to 60 minutes, or until a cake tester inserted in the centre comes out clean. If the bread begins to brown too quickly, tent it with foil after 45 minutes in the oven.

When the bread test is done, remove it from the oven and place on a cooling rack; after 15 minutes, remove the bread from its pan and place back on the rack to finish cooling. Slice when it has cooled completely. Store at room temperature in a bread bag or airtight container for up to 4 to 5 days.

Saskatoon Berry Jam Rolls

Ingredients

4-1/2 Cups all-purpose flour sifted

3/4 Cup cake flour, sifted

2-1/4 Teaspoons (1 envelope, or 8 g) instant dry yeast

1/2 Teaspoon salt

4 Tablespoons white sugar

2 Cups milk, lukewarm

3 Eggs

1 Teaspoon vanilla extract

1/2 Cup vegetable oil

Orange zest from one orange

1 Cup mixed berry jam

1/4 Cup butter (for brushing between buns and baking pan)

1 Egg for egg wash

Powdered sugar (optional)

Directions

Combine all the dry ingredients, flour, cake flour, instant dry yeast, sugar, and salt. Give it a light swirl then add lukewarm water, vanilla extract, vegetable oil and the orange zest. Knead this by hand or use a mixer, until your dough becomes smooth and just a little bit sticky. Place the dough in an oiled bowl and let it rest in a warm place.

Punch down the dough and roll out onto a lightly floured surface. Roll it out so that it's a big rectangle about 14 inches by 18 inches. It should be about 1/2 inch in thickness. Using some sort of kitchen tool, cut the dough into 2-3/4x2-3/4-inch squares.

Make a small indentation into each square and place about 1 teaspoon of jam in the centre. Carefully fold each square in half and pinch the ends together. If your dough is not a bit sticky…you are in trouble.

Place them onto a buttered pan and brush some more butter on the sides of the rolls, so that they don't stick together. Brush them with some egg wash as well then let them sit for another 20 minutes or so to rise a bit more.

Preheat oven to 350°F (175°C). Bake them for about 25 to 30 minutes, until nice and golden brown.

Serve sprinkled with some powdered sugar.

Saskatoon Berry and Honey Sticky Biscuits

Ingredients

<u>Filling</u>

1 Cup Saskatoon berries

1/4 Cup honey (plus extra, if you like)

<u>Stickiness</u>

2 Tablespoons butter

2 Tablespoons packed brown sugar

3 Tablespoons honey

<u>Biscuits</u>

2 Cups flour

1 Tablespoons baking powder

1 Tablespoons sugar

1/4 Teaspoon salt

3/4 Cup milk

1/4 Cup canola oil

Directions

<u>Filling</u>

Simmer the Saskatoon berries and honey in a small saucepan over medium heat until the berries burst. Set aside to cool slightly.

<u>Biscuit</u>

Put the butter, brown sugar, and honey into an 8"x8" pan that has been sprayed with non-stick spray, put it in the oven and turn it on to 350°F.

In a large bowl, combine flour, baking powder, sugar, and salt. Add the milk and canola oil and stir by hand just until you have a soft dough. Do not overmix!

On a lightly floured surface, pat or roll the dough into a 9"x14" rectangle. Spread with the cooled saskatoon berry mixture. If you like, drizzle with a little extra honey.

Starting from a long side, roll tightly jelly-roll style into a log. Cut into 9 biscuits using dental floss or a serrated knife, and place cut side down in the pan.

Bake for 20 minutes, until golden and bubbly. Invert onto a platter while still warm.

Saskatoon Poppy Seed Loaf

Ingredients

2 Cups Saskatoon berries

2 Tablespoons Cassis® liqueur

3/4 Cup sugar

2 Cups all-purpose flour

2 Teaspoons baking powder

2 Tablespoons poppy seeds

1/4 Teaspoon sea salt

8 (4 ounces or 115 grams) Tablespoons unsalted butter, room temperature

1 Teaspoon finely grated lemon zest

1 Tablespoon lemon juice

3 Extra large eggs, room temperature

1/3 Cup sliced almonds

1 – 9"x5"x3" non-stick loaf pan – buttered, lined with wax paper and buttered again

Directions

Preheat oven to 350°F (180°C).

Place the berries, liqueur and 1/4 cup of sugar in a medium bowl. Stir well and set aside.

Place the flour, 1/4 cup of sugar, baking powder, poppy seeds, and salt in a medium bowl. Stir well and set aside.

Place the soft butter, 1/4 cup sugar, lemon zest, and lemon juice in the bowl of an electric mixer. Beat at slow speed until creamy. Add the eggs one at a time and beat at medium speed until well incorporated and smooth. Add the flour mixture and gently fold in with a wooden spoon until barely incorporated. Add the berry mixture and fold until just moistened.

Spoon the batter into the prepared mould. Garnish with the almond slices. Bake for 65 to 70 minutes until golden and toothpick inserted in centre comes out clean. Remove from oven and let cool for 10 minutes before un-moulding. Loosen the cake by gently pulling up on the wax paper and then lift it from pan. Cool on racks until warm or room temperature, then peel off the wax paper.

Saskatoon Berry Bread Braid

Ingredients

1 Cup milk

1 Egg beaten

1 Tablespoon butter or margarine

3 Tablespoons sugar

3-1/3 Cups flour

<u>Saskatoon Filling</u>

3/4 Teaspoon yeast

1/3 Cup water

1 Tablespoon lemon juice

1 Cup fresh Saskatoon berries

1/4 Cup sugar

2 Tablespoons cornstarch

Directions

Add the milk to the bread machine. Check your instructions for your own bread machine. This recipe does wet first. Beat egg and throw it into the milk. Add the butter. then the flour and yeast. Use your pasta/dough setting.

Bring the water and lemon juice to a boil in the pot. Once it's boiling, add your Saskatoons and bring to a boil again. Turn down the heat on the burner at this point.

Whisk together your sugar and cornstarch, then add to the pot. Stir constantly until the mixture is clear, and it does clear up. Put in the fridge to cool.

When the dough is ready, Put it on a lightly floured surface. Separate into two pieces, roll them into two rectangles that are about 14"x9". Spread your pie filling in the middle.

Criss-cross the dough until the filling is covered and place on a greased sheet. Brush with melted butter. Cover, and let them rise until they look like puffy.

Preheat your oven to 350°F and bake until they are golden brown.

Breakfast

Saskatoon Berry Lentil Muffin

Ingredients

1-1/2 Cups large green lentils, cooked

1/2 Cup orange juice

2 Cups all-purpose flour

1 Tablespoon baking powder

1/2 Teaspoon salt

1/2 Teaspoon cinnamon

1/2 Teaspoon ground allspice

1/2 Teaspoon pumpkin pie spice

1/2 Cup honey

1/2 Cup canola oil

2 Eggs

1-3/4 cups fresh Saskatoon berries

Directions

Preheat oven to 400°F (200°C).

In a blender, combine 1/2 cup lentils and 1/4 cup orange juice. Purée until smooth.

Sift together flour, baking powder, salt, cinnamon, allspice, and pumpkin pie spice.

In a separate bowl, mix together lentil purée, remaining lentils, remaining orange juice, honey, oil, eggs, and Saskatoon berries. Add to dry mixture stirring only until dry ingredients are moistened. Spoon mixture into paper-lined muffin cups, filling 3/4 full.

Bake 20 to 25 minutes or until a toothpick inserted in centre comes out clean.

Summer Berries with Orange Cream Topping

Ingredients

1 Teaspoon finely shredded orange peel (set aside)

2 Tablespoons orange juice

1 Tablespoon orange liqueur or orange juice

1 Tablespoon honey

1 Teaspoon white or regular balsamic vinegar

6 Cups assorted fresh berries (such as blueberries, Saskatoon berries, blackberries, red and/or golden raspberries, and/or halved small strawberries)

3/4 Cup frozen sugar-free or light whipped dessert topping, thawed

1/2 Cup light sour cream

Thinly sliced kumquats (optional)

Directions

Marinade

In a screw-top jar, combine orange juice, liqueur, honey, and balsamic vinegar. Cover and shake well.

Place berries in a large bowl. Pour marinade over berries. Toss gently to coat. Cover and chill in the refrigerator for 1 to 3 hours, tossing occasionally.

Cream Topping

In a small bowl, fold together dessert topping, sour cream, and orange peel.

To serve, top berries with the cream topping. If desired, garnish with kumquats. Makes 12 servings (1/2 cup berries and 1-1/2 tablespoons cream topping each).

White Chocolate Saskatoon Berry Scones

Ingredients

1 Cup of sour cream

1 Teaspoon baking soda

4 Cups of flour

1 Cup of white sugar

1-1/2 Cups of Saskatoon berries

1 Package of white chocolate chips

1 Cup of butter

1 Egg

2 Teaspoon baking powder

1 Teaspoon salt

Directions

Preheat oven to 350°F.

In a small bowl combine the sour cream and baking soda together, this is going to poof up while you are mixing the rest of the recipe up.

In a large mixing bowl, whisk together the flour, sugar, baking powder and salt. Cut in the butter using two knives scissor style or with a pastry blender until it resembles coarse peas in the flour mixture. Add the sour cream and beaten egg, gently mixing until it's almost together. Once the mixture is close to being completely combined, add in the bag of white chocolate chips. Mix gently again. Once well-mixed, add in the Saskatoon berries.

The mixture should now be scooped together and rolled it into one large log. Cut the log into three pieces. Flatten each round disk into a 6-inch square then cut into 6 equal triangles. Take your 18 scones and place on a well-greased cookie sheet or parchment lined cookie sheet. Bake at 350°F until browned and beautiful, about 20 minutes.

‡ Makes 18 scones.

Blueberry-Carrot-Saskatoon Berry Bran Muffins

Ingredients

2 Cups wheat bran

1 Cup oat bran

1 Cup whole wheat flour

2 Teaspoons baking soda

1 Teaspoon baking powder

1/3 Teaspoon salt

2 Large eggs

2/3 Cup unsweetened almond milk

2/3 Cup plain Greek yoghurt

1/2 Cup unsweetened applesauce

1/4 Cup virgin coconut oil

1 Tablespoon chia seeds

1 Tablespoon ground flaxseed

1 Tablespoon shelled hemp seeds (Shelled)

1-1/2 Cups blueberries

1/2 Cup berries (Saskatoon, Or Cranberries)

2/3 Packet Stevia® (Pure, 1/2 teaspoon)

3 Carrots (Shredded Small)

Directions

Preheat oven to 350°F. Mix all ingredients together in one large bowl. Make sure to melt coconut oil before stirring in. Pour into muffin tins and bake for 15 minutes or until middle is done.

Saskatoon Berry Filled Chocolate Crepe Cups

Ingredients

1/2 Cup all-purpose flour

2 Teaspoons unsweetened cocoa powder

1/8 Teaspoon salt

1 Egg

3/4 Cup fat-free milk

1 Tablespoon cooking oil

Non-stick cooking spray

1/2 Cup frozen fat-free whipped dessert topping, thawed

1/2 Cup raspberry fat-free yoghurt with no-calorie sweetener

20 Fresh Saskatoon berries

Fresh mint leaves (optional)

Directions

Preheat oven to 400°F. In a small bowl, stir together flour, cocoa powder, and salt; set aside. In a medium bowl, lightly beat egg with a wire whisk. Whisk in milk, oil, and flour mixture until combined.

Lightly coat an unheated non-stick griddle and twenty 1-3/4-inch muffin cups with non-stick cooking spray; set muffin cups aside. Preheat griddle over medium heat. For each crepe, spoon 1 tablespoon of the batter onto griddle (hold spoon close to griddle when spooning and pour slowly to make circles). Cook for 30 to 60 seconds or until bottom is golden brown and top appears dry. (You can cook multiple crepes at a time.) Use a spatula to remove crepes to paper towels, browned sides up. Repeat with remaining batter. If desired, when cool enough to handle, trim edges of crepes. Gently press crepes, browned sides down, into prepared muffin cups, pleating as necessary to fit.

Bake crepe cups about 12 minutes or until edges are browned and crepes appear to hold their shapes. Cool in muffin cups on wire racks. Carefully remove from muffin cups.

In a medium bowl, fold together whipped dessert topping and yoghurt. Cover with foil or plastic wrap and chill until ready to use or up to 24 hours.

Just before serving, spoon yoghurt mixture into crepe cups. Top each cup with a berry. If desired, garnish with fresh mint leaves.

‡ Makes 20 crepe cups.

Saskatoon Smoothie

Ingredients

1 Cup Saskatoon berries

1 Cup skim milk

1/2 Cup plain yoghurt

1 Banana, cut into chunks

1/2 Cup pineapple, crushed

1 Tablespoon flax seed, crushed

Directions

Combine all ingredients in blender container. Process for 2 minutes or until smooth.

White Chocolate Saskatoon Berry Muffins

Ingredients

1-3/4 Cup all-purpose flour

3 Tablespoons baking powder

1/2 Teaspoon salt

1/2 Cup granulated sugar

1/4 Cup melted butter

1 Egg

3/4 Cup milk

1 Teaspoon vanilla

1 Cup Saskatoon berries

1/2 Cup of white chocolate chips

Directions

Pre-heat your oven to 400°F.

In a large bowl whisk together, the dry ingredients. Combine the milk. beaten egg, vanilla, and butter in a small bowl. Pour the liquid into the dry ingredients and mix until just combined. Stir in the Saskatoons and white chocolate chips gently.

Divide the batter between 12 lined muffin tins.

Bake at 400°F for 20 to 25 minutes, until browned on top. Cool on wire rack.

Whole Wheat Saskatoon Muffins

Ingredients

2 Cups whole wheat flour

2-1/2 Teaspoon baking powder

1/4 Teaspoon salt

1 Teaspoon cinnamon

1-1/2 Cups Saskatoons

1/2 Cup brown sugar

1/4 Cup canola oil

3/4 Cup skim milk

2 Egg whites

1/2 Teaspoon vanilla

Directions

Preheat oven to 375°F.

In a bowl, mix flour, baking powder, salt, and cinnamon. In a separate bowl, combine egg whites, canola oil, skim milk and vanilla. Add brown sugar and stir until dissolved. Stir in Saskatoons. Add liquid ingredients to dry ingredients and stir only until well moistened.

Fill 12 greased or paper lined muffin tins. Bake at 375°F for 16 minutes or until evenly browned.

‡ Makes 12.

Brownies, Squares, and More

Saskatoon Berry and Apple Sauce Bars

Ingredients

1/4 Cup margarine, butter, or oil

2/3 Cup brown sugar

1 Egg

1 Cup applesauce

1 Cup Flour

1 Teaspoon baking soda

1/2 Teaspoon cinnamon

1/4 Teaspoon ground ginger

1/4 Teaspoon ground allspice

1/4 Teaspoon sea salt

1/4-1/2 Cup Saskatoon berries

2 Tablespoons powdered icing sugar, for dusting on top

Directions

Preheat oven to 350°F (180°C). Cream together margarine and brown sugar. Blend in egg. In a separate bowl, combine dry ingredients. Stir dry mixture into wet ingredients. Fold in berries.

Into a greased 2-quart square or rectangular baking dish, pour batter and spread out evenly. Bake for about 25 minutes, or until the middle of pan tests done. Be careful not to overbake. Cool bars in the pan. Cut into squares or rectangles and dust with powdered sugar just prior to serving.

Saskatoon Berry Butter Tarts

Ingredients

Saskatoon Berry Pie Filling

4 Cups Saskatoon berries

1/4 Cup water

2 Tablespoons fresh lemon juice

3/4 Cup sugar

3 Tablespoons cornstarch

Butter Tart Filling

2 Eggs

1/3 Cup butter

1 Cup white sugar

1 Teaspoon vanilla

4 Tablespoons cream

1 Cup raisins seedless

Pie Crust

2 Cups flour

1/2 Teaspoon salt

2/3 Cup shortening lard

1/4 Cup water

Directions

Saskatoon Berry Filling

In a saucepan, mix together the berries and water and simmer for 10 minutes over low-medium heat. In a separate bowl, mix together the sugar and flour. Then add the sugar/flour mix to the berries and combine. Simmer until the mixture slightly thickens. Set aside to cool.

Butter Tart Filling

First beat together the eggs.

In a saucepan, melt the butter. Then add the sugar, vanilla, cream, raisins and beaten eggs to the saucepan and bring to a boil over medium heat, and boil for 3 minutes. Set aside.

Pie Crust

Sift flour and salt into a bowl. Cut in shortening until the particles are pea-sized with a pie cutter. Sprinkle in water, 1 teaspoon or so at a time, mixing lightly with a fork. Don't over mix or the crust will be tough. Press into a ball. It is okay if it is crumbly because it makes for a tender, flaky crust!

Final

Preheat your oven to 375°F.

Split the pie dough into 2 balls, then using a rolling pin, roll out each ball, doing one at a time (it's just easier to handle the dough this way).

Using a 3-inch circle (like a drinking glass, or cookie cutter), cut out your tart shells.

Place the tart shells into a muffin tin. Add a heaping tablespoon of the butter tart mixture into the shell, then add a tablespoon of the Saskatoon pie filling on top of the butter tart filling. Do not mix. Bake for 18 to 20 minutes, or until the crust is slightly browned.

Saskatoon Berry Napoleon

Ingredients

1 Package of puff pastry

Pastry Cream

1-1/4 Cups of milk

1/4 Cup of granulated sugar

1 Teaspoon of vanilla

3 Egg yolks

2-1/2 Tablespoons of cornstarch

Saskatoon Berry Filling

2 Cups of fresh or frozen Saskatoon berries

1/4 Cup of granulated sugar

1/2 Cup of water

1-1/2 Tablespoons of cornstarch

Whipped Cream

1 Small carton of whipping cream

2 Tablespoons of granulated sugar

Directions

Preheat oven to 400°F.

Unroll your thawed puff pastry. If the pastry is not pre-rolled roll it out, on a lightly floured surface, to 1/4-inch thickness.

Use cookie cutter. Place cut pastry on a cookie sheet lined with a baking liner or parchment paper. Place in the oven and cook for 10-15 minutes or until puffed up and golden brown. Remove from oven and move the pastry to a wire rack to cool.

<u>Pastry Cream</u>

Pour milk and vanilla into a saucepan and heat over medium/low heat until it just starts to steam. Remove from heat.

In a medium-sized bowl whisk together the egg yolks, sugar and cornstarch. Slowly pour the warm milk into the egg mixture, whisking the entire time. Pour this mixture back into the pan and heat over medium/low heat, stirring constantly, until the becomes very thick. Remove from heat, place into a small bowl, and put in the fridge to chill.

<u>Saskatoon Berry Sauce</u>

Place the water and sugar in a saucepan and heat over medium/high heat until boiling. Add the Saskatoons and let boil again. Once it starts to boil reduce heat to low and simmer for 10 minutes. Slowly add the cornstarch and, stirring constantly, cook for a few more minutes until the sauce thickens. Place in a small bowl and put in the fridge to chill.

<u>Whipped Cream</u>

Beat the whipping cream in a deep bowl until peaks form. Add the sugar and beat for 1 more minute. Set in fridge until needed.

<u>Napoleons</u>

Using a sharp serrated knife cut your pasty in half lengthwise. Spread a generous layer of pastry cream on the bottom half of your pastry. Follow with a layer of berry filling and a layer of whipped cream. Place top half of the pastry over your layers.

Saskatoon Berry Strudel

Ingredients

3 Frozen patty shells

3 Cups Saskatoon berry pie filling

3 Tablespoons melted butter

1 Tablespoon ground almond coarse sugar granules

Directions

Press edges of patty shell together; roll out on a floured cloth to 18x14-inch rectangle. In a teacup, combine melted butter and ground almond. Place pie filling evenly along side of the rectangle, about 4 inches from the edge. Without stretching, carefully fold the 4-inch piece of dough over the filling. Pick up the cloth, making the dough roll forward into a tight roll. Seal ends. Place on a foil-lined baking sheet; curve strudel, forming a crescent or horseshoe shape. Brush on almond-butter mixture over the top of strudel. Lightly sprinkle the sugar granules over the strudel.

Bake in 350°F oven for 45 to 50 minutes. Remove from sheet; cool on a rack.

‡ Makes 6 servings.

Saskatoon Berry Galette

Ingredients

<u>Galette</u>

1 or 2 Packages of frozen pastry

2 Cups of fresh Saskatoon berries

2 Tablespoons of white sugar

2 Tablespoons of flour

Fresh lemon zest (a couple of rasps)

Egg yolk or heavy cream for brushing pastry

Light brown sugar for sprinkling over the pastry

<u>Raspberry Crunch Topping</u>

1/2 Cup of slow cooking rolled oats or granola

1 Tablespoon of butter

1 Tablespoon of flour (a little more if you use granola to absorb the raspberry liquid)

1/3 Cup of fresh raspberries

Directions

<u>Raspberry Crunch Topping</u>

Mix all ingredients together; consistency should be that of the topping for an apple crisp (If there is a lot of liquid from the raspberries, let it sit a bit for the oats to soak it up, or add a bit of flour to absorb it).

<u>Galette</u>

Pre-heat the oven to 400°F. Roll out the pastry and cut into 6 discs.

Mix all filling ingredients together and divide evenly onto the discs. Fold pastry up over the filling and secure by pinching to ensure the berries are enveloped tightly.

Brush each Galette with egg yolk or heavy cream. Sprinkle with the light brown sugar. Place a teaspoon of raspberry crunch on top of each. Bake for 25 minutes; cool for 5 minutes and serve warm with ice cream.

‡ Makes 6 Galette.

Cakes

Saskatoon Berry Cream Cheese Crumb Cake

Ingredients

<u>Crumb Layer</u>

1-1/2 Cups brown sugar

1-1/2 Cups all-purpose flour

1 Cup rolled oats

1-1/2 Teaspoons ground cinnamon

2/3 Cup vegetable oil

<u>Berry Layer</u>

5 Cups fresh Saskatoon berries

1/3 Cup water

2 Tablespoons lemon juice

3/4 Cup white sugar

2 Tablespoons all-purpose flour

<u>Cream Cheese Layer</u>

1 (4 ounce) Package cream cheese, diced

Directions

Preheat oven to 350°F (175°C). Grease an 8-inch square baking pan.

Whisk brown sugar, 1-1/2 cups flour, oats, and cinnamon together in a bowl; gradually stir in oil until mixture is crumbly. Press half the crumb mixture into the prepared pan; set remaining crumbs aside for topping.

Bake in the preheated oven until firm, about 10 minutes. Remove crust from oven and cool slightly, leaving the oven on.

Place Saskatoon berries and water in a saucepan. Bring to a simmer and cook for 10 minutes; stir in lemon juice. Whisk white sugar and 2 tablespoons flour together in a small bowl; stir sugar mixture into berries and cook until the mixture begins to thicken about 3 minutes. Allow to cool for a few minutes; pour berry filling over crumb crust.

Sprinkle cream cheese pieces evenly over berry filling. Spread remaining crumb mixture over cream cheese layer and press gently with a potato masher.

Bake in the preheated oven until crumb topping is golden and filling is bubbly about 40 minutes.

Whole Wheat Saskatoon Berry Shortcake

Ingredients

Shortcake

1 Cup flour

1 Cup whole wheat flour

1/4 Cup sugar

2 Teaspoon baking powder

1/3 Cup cold butter, cut into small cubes

1 Large egg

1 Teaspoon vanilla extract

1/2 Cup milk

Sugar for sprinkling

Whipped Cream

1 Cup whipping cream

1 Teaspoon sugar

Saskatoon Berry Compote

2 Cup Saskatoons

1-1/2 Cup sugar

Directions

Shortcake

In a bowl sift together flours, sugar and baking powder. Cut in butter with a fork or pastry cutter until it looks crumbly. Mix together wet ingredients. Form a well in the centre of dry ingredients and pour in wet ingredients, slowly mixing together. Knead together and transfer to a floured surface, kneading and stretching a few times. Form into a rectangle approximately 6"x9" for a small size. Form the dough into 4"x 7" and cut into six pieces for larger, thicker pieces. Sprinkle tops with sugar and bake at 400°F for 15-20 minutes until golden brown. Let cool.

Whipping Cream

In an electric mixer beat the cream and sugar on high until soft peaks form. Don't overbeat. Can do this by hand, it'll just take a while longer.

Saskatoon Berry Compote

In a medium saucepan over medium-high heat bring Saskatoons and sugar to a boil, stirring constantly throughout. Let simmer for a minute or two then transfer to a bowl and let cool, it should thicken up quite a bit.

Cut shortcakes in half and layer on whipped cream and Saskatoons to serve.

Polka-Dot Angel Cupcakes

Ingredients

1-1/2 Cups egg whites (10 to 12)

1 Cup sifted cake flour

1/2 Cup sugar

1 1/2 Teaspoons cream of tartar

1 Teaspoon vanilla

1/2 Teaspoon almond extract

1/2 Teaspoon salt

3/4 Cup sugar

1 Cup Saskatoon berries, diced

Directions

In a very large mixing bowl allow egg whites to stand at room temperature for 30 minutes. Meanwhile, sift cake flour and 1/2 cup sugar together 3 times; set aside. Grease 12 popover pans, if using. Line popover pans or 12 jumbo (3-1/4-inch) muffin cups with large paper bake cups. Preheat oven to 350°F.

Add cream of tartar, vanilla, almond extract, and salt to egg whites. Beat with an electric mixer on medium speed until soft peaks form (tips curl). Gradually add 3/4 cup sugar, about 2 tablespoons at a time, beating until stiff peaks form (tips stand straight).

Sift one-fourth of the cake flour mixture over beaten egg whites; fold in gently. Repeat, folding in the remaining flour mixture by fourths.

Spoon half of the batter into the popover pans or muffin cups, filling about half full. Sprinkle a few berry pieces onto each, then top with another large dollop of batter and remaining berries. Mound remaining batter over fruit pieces (the cups will be very full).

Bake for 15 to 18 minutes or until the tops are golden brown and spring back when lightly touched with a finger. Cool the cupcakes on a wire rack in the pan. To remove, run a knife around edges. If desired, wrap with new paper bake cups and tie with ribbon.

‡ Makes 12 cupcakes.

Gluten-Free Saskatoon Berry Cheesecake

Ingredients

1-3/4 Cup gluten-free graham crumbs

1/4 Cup melted butter

3 Cups Saskatoon berries

1/2 Cup sugar

3 Tablespoon cornstarch

2 Packages cream cheese

1/4 Cup sugar

1 Teaspoon vanilla

1 Cup whipping cream

Directions

<u>Crust</u>

Heat oven to 350°F. Add gluten-free graham crumbs and melted butter to the square dish. Stir to mix and then spread evenly. Pat down for an even crust. Place dish (9 X 9 glass dish works best) in the oven for 8 to 10 minutes. Remove from oven and let crust cool.

<u>Filling</u>

Beat cream cheese until smooth, then slowly add sugar and vanilla. Beat mixture until well blended.

In a clean bowl, beat the whipping cream until soft peaks form. Slowly beat the whipped cream into the cream cheese mixture. Spoon the cream cheese/whipping cream mixture onto the cooled graham crust. Smooth filling onto crust.

Berry Topping

In a large saucepan heat, 3 cups Saskatoon berries with 2-1/2 to 3 cups water until mixture starts to come to a boil. Reduce heat to medium.

In a small bowl mix the 3 tablespoons cornstarch with 3 tablespoons cold water. Stir until smooth. Add cornstarch mixture to hot berries and slowly stir until mixture thickens.

Remove from heat and let cool. Berries will thicken further as they cool.

Once cool top cream cheese mixture with berries. Cover with saran wrap and completely cool in refrigerator. Slice and serve.

Vanilla Saskatoon Meringue Cupcakes

Ingredients

Cake

1 Cup sugar

1-3/4 Cups cake flour (not all-purpose)

1-1/2 Teaspoons baking powder

1/2 Teaspoon baking soda

1/2 Teaspoon salt

1/4 Cup unsalted butter

2 Large eggs (or 4 egg yolks from the meringue for a yellow cake)

1/3 Cup sour cream

1/4 Cup canola oil

1 Tablespoon pure vanilla extract

2/3 Cup (160 ml) whole milk

Meringue

4 Egg whites

1 cup sugar

Directions

Cake

Preheat oven to 350°F. Mix wet and dry ingredients separately and then 1 third at a time mix the dry into the wet. This is a liquid cake batter. Pour the batter into a large Ziploc® and snip off one corner. Use the bag as a piping bag and fill your cupcake liners a little more than half full. Bake for 14 minutes and then test to see if they are done. Test with toothpick. The cupcakes should be white, not golden brown. If they are not quite done check at two-minute intervals until they are. If they turn brown they will be overcooked. When the cupcakes are done be sure to remove them from the tins to cool. This will prevent overcooking.

Meringue

Use your stand mixer bowl if you have one, over a double boiler. Whisk the eggs and sugar together until they become frothy and no longer have any grit. Attach the bowl to the mixer and with the whisk attachment, whisk at top speed until stiff peaks form. You know you have stiff peaks if you can slide all the meringue to one side and it stays. For better meringue, be sure to quickly wipe the bowl and whisk with vinegar to eliminate any grease or oil that may be there.

To add the Saskatoon filling to the cupcake, use a serrated knife to cut a hole in the top for the filling to go in. Fill it as full as you can without it dripping over the edges and then pipe using your 1M tip around the filling.

Saskatoon Berry Coffee Cake

Ingredients

1 Cup sugar

1/2 Cup butter or margarine

2 Eggs

2 Cups whole wheat flour

1 Teaspoon baking powder

1/2 Teaspoon baking soda

1/4 Teaspoon salt

1 Cup plain yoghurt or sour cream

1 Cup Saskatoon berries

Filling

3 Tablespoon brown sugar

1 Teaspoon cinnamon

1/2 Cup chopped walnuts

Directions

Cream together sugar and butter, add eggs and beat well.

Combine flour, baking powder, soda and salt and add alternately with yoghurt.

When well blended, add Saskatoon berries and stir gently.

Spoon half of the mixture into a well-greased pan (Bundt, ring mould or 9" square), sprinkle with nut mixture and top with remaining batter.

Bake at 350°F for 40 minutes. When slightly cool, sprinkle with icing sugar and lemon rind.

Candies and Chocolates

Saskatoon Berry Fudge

Ingredients

1/2 Cup coconut oil

1/2 Cup creamed honey

3/4 Cup cocoa powder

1 Teaspoon vanilla extract

1 Cup Saskatoon berries

Directions

In a small saucepan over low heat, gently cook the Saskatoon berries with a splash of water until they are soft and tender. Remove from heat and allow to cool. In a food processor, blend coconut oil and honey until creamed together. Add vanilla, cocoa and berries, processing until smooth. Pour the fudge onto plastic wrap placed on top of a cookie sheet.

Gently wrap it up so that it forms a loose rectangle approximately 1/2 to 3/4" thick. Place it in the freezer for four hours or longer. Should solidify nicely in under two hours. Unwrap, cut into squares, and store the leftovers in the fridge to maintain firmness.

Saskatoon Berry Lollipops

Ingredients

Vegetable oil, for brushing

1 Cup sugar

1/2 Cup water

1/3 Cup light corn syrup

1/4 Cup Saskatoon berry concentrate

4 Drops red food colouring

24 6-Inch lollipop sticks

Directions

Brush 2 flat baking sheets with oil. Fill a pie plate with 1 inch of cold water.

In a small, heavy saucepan, combine the sugar, water and corn syrup and bring to a boil, stirring just until the sugar dissolves. Boil over high heat, without stirring, until the syrup reaches 280°F on a candy thermometer, about 20 minutes. Add the Saskatoon berry concentrate and food colouring and cook over moderately high heat until the syrup reaches 300°F. Briefly, dip the saucepan in the cold water to stop the cooking.

Once the bubbling subsides, carefully spoon 6 scant tablespoons of syrup about 2 inches apart on 1 of the prepared baking sheets. Working quickly, place a stick in each of the lollipops, turning it to cover with syrup. Continue to form the lollipops, 6 at a time, until both baking sheets are full. If the syrup in the saucepan becomes too thick, melt it over low heat. Let the lollipops harden, then wrap in plastic.

Fresh Fruit Chocolate Bar

Ingredients

1/2 Banana

4 Large strawberries

10 Saskatoon berries

2 Cups bittersweet chocolate chips

Equipment: mini loaf pan, foil, cooking spray

Directions

Prepare the fruit, slicing the banana and strawberries into thin 1/4" slices. Slice the raspberries and blackberries into 1/4" slices. Cut Saskatoon berries in half.

Melt the chocolate chips in the microwave, 30 seconds at a time, stirring each time, until smooth and completely melted.

Line the loaf pan with strips of foil so that it overhangs on each side. Spritz with a bit of cooking spray so that it peels off easily.

Spread a thin 1/2" layer of chocolate in the bottom of each well. Arrange the prepared fruit closely together. Top off with another thin layer of chocolate. Tap the pan against the table so that everything settles and to get rid of any air bubbles. Add additional chocolate to any parts where fruit peeks out.

Place in refrigerator and let chill 30 minutes or until chocolate is completely set. Use a warm knife to loosen the edges and then lift out of the mould. Peel off the foil and serve immediately or store in the fridge wrapped in foil up to 24 hours.

‡ Makes 4 chocolate bars.

Chocolate Covered Saskatoon Berries

Ingredients

1 Pint fresh Saskatoon berries

1 Bag (2 cups) semi-sweet or dark chocolate chips

1 Teaspoon coconut oil or shortening (such as Crisco®)

Directions

Wash Saskatoon berries and then dry well by blotting and then spreading out on a paper towel-lined baking sheet and letting sit for about 1 hour. You want to make sure that no water is left on the outside of the berries as that will cause the chocolate to "seize" and not coat the berries well.

Prepare a baking sheet by lining it with wax paper. Once the berries are dry, combine the chocolate and the coconut oil or shortening, and melt in the microwave in 30-second intervals until smooth, using a spoon to stir in between 30 seconds. Will typically take about 1 minute to 90 seconds total.

Add a few berries to the chocolate at a time and stir to coat, then place on the baking sheet with a spoon. You can place them individually or in small clumps of 2 to 5 for larger pieces. Repeat with rest of berries and chocolate.

Place in the refrigerator for about 10 minutes to set. Serve immediately and store any uneaten chocolates in an airtight bag in the fridge for up to 3 days.

Cookies

Saskatoon Berry Shortbread

Ingredients

1 Cup margarine

1/2 Cup honey

2 Cups all-purpose flour

1 Egg white

2 Cups Saskatoon berries

2 Tablespoons honey

1 Tablespoon all-purpose flour

2 Cups sliced almonds

Directions

Whip margarine and 1/2 cup of honey together. Gradually add 2 cups of flour while continuing to beat. Beat the egg white with 1 to 2 tablespoons of water. Form balls of dough from the margarine, honey, flour mixture and roll them in the egg white mixture, and then in sliced almonds to coat.

Place them on a greased cookie sheet and make an indent in the centre with your thumb. Bake at 375°F (190°C) for 12 to 15 minutes. Reshape the indent while they are cooling, if necessary.

Combine the fresh or frozen Saskatoon berries with 4 tablespoons of water and the 2 tablespoons of honey in a saucepan. Heat until honey has melted. Mash the Saskatoons a little. Add up to 1 tablespoon flour as needed to thicken into a jam-like consistency.

Put about 1 teaspoon of filling into the indent of each cookie.

‡ Makes 12-15 cookies.

Saskatoon Berry Cookies

Ingredients

1/2 Cup butter, room temp

2/3 Cup brown sugar

1 Egg

1/4 Cup light sour cream

1 Cup whole wheat flour

1 Cup all-purpose flour

2 Teaspoon baking powder

Pinch salt

1 Cup Saskatoons

Directions

Preheat oven to 350°F. Line a cookie sheet with parchment paper.

In a large bowl, cream together butter and brown sugar until creamy. Add egg and beat until combined. Beat in sour cream.

In a medium bowl, whisk together whole wheat flour, flour, baking powder, and salt.

Beat dry ingredients into wet ingredients until just combined. Gently fold in saskatoons.

Drop by the tablespoonful onto prepared cookie sheet (or use a small cookie scoop), about an inch apart.

Bake at 350°F for 10 to 15 minutes. Tops should be light brown.

Remove from oven and let cool on cookie sheet for 5 minutes before removing to wire rack to cool completely.

Saskatoon Berry Oatmeal Cookies

Ingredients

3/4 Cup butter

3/4 Cup brown sugar

1/4 Cup white sugar

1 Egg

1 Tablespoon milk

1 Teaspoon Almond extract

1-1/4 Cup flour

1 Teaspoon cinnamon

1 Teaspoon baking soda

1/4 Teaspoon salt

2-1/2 Cups rolled oats

1/4 Cup medium unsweetened coconut

1-1/2 Cups Saskatoon berries

Directions

Using an electric mixer, combine butter, sugars, egg, milk, and almond extract until light and fluffy.

Whisk together the flour, cinnamon, baking soda, and salt and add to the butter mixture.

Add the rolled oats and coconut, mix thoroughly and then very gently stir in the Saskatoon berries. Be careful not to break them. You don't want purple cookie dough!

Place the dough in the fridge for 1 hour, then drop by spoonfuls on to parchment paper lined cookie sheet. Bake at 350°F for 12 to 14 minutes.

Saskatoon Macaroons

Ingredients

1 14-Ounce can sweetened condensed milk

1 Teaspoon vanilla extract

1 14-Ounce bag sweetened shredded coconut

2 Large egg whites

1/4 Teaspoon kosher salt

3/4 Cups saskatoon jam (approx.)

Directions

Preheat oven to 350°F. line a baking sheet with parchment set it aside.

In a large bowl, combine 1 cup of the condensed milk and vanilla. Mix in the coconut and set aside.

In a separate bowl, beat the egg whites and salt until stiff peaks form. Fold the egg mixture into the coconut mixture and then spoon balls of it onto the baking sheet (1-1/2-inch balls).

Bake for 20 to 25 minutes (more if they're larger), until they become golden brown. Let cool and then spoon a teaspoon of jam onto the tops.

Fillings, Frostings, and Topping

Saskatoon Berry Perogy Filling

Ingredients

Filling

2/3 Cup sugar

1 Tablespoon all-purpose flour

2 Cups fresh or frozen (don't thaw them) Saskatoon berries

Perogy Dough

5 Cups all-purpose flour

1 Teaspoon salt

1/2 Cup canola oil

1 Large egg

2 Cups very hot, boiled water

Directions

Filling

In a medium bowl, stir together the sugar and flour; stir in the blueberries or Saskatoon berries. If they're frozen, store in the freezer until you're ready to use them.

‡ Makes enough for about 3 dozen perogies.

Perogy Dough

In a large bowl mix together, the flour and salt.

Whisk the oil and egg together in a measuring cup; add to the flour and stir until you have a coarse meal, like biscuit dough before you add the liquid.

Add the water all at once and immediately stir – it will look lumpy and ugly and as if there isn't enough moisture to go around. Keep at it, stir with your hands if you must, and the dough will come together. Let it sit for 15 to 30 minutes.

Roll out on a lightly floured surface and cut circles with the rim of a drinking glass or perogy cutter. Fill with the Saskatoon berry filling and seal.

Saskatoon Berry Syrup

Ingredients

4 Cups serviceberries

1 Cup water

1 Cup granulated sugar

Directions

Add the water to the serviceberries in a saucepan and crush. I used a potato masher.

Slowly bring to the boil over medium-high heat and simmer for about 10 minutes. Allow to cool a little and then strain through a jelly bag or muslin. This yields about 1 cup of juice.

Add 1 cup of sugar to the cup of juice and heat over medium heat until the sugar is dissolved, and the sauce has thickened a little. Do not let it boil.

Once it is cool pour it into a jar or bottle and it will keep in the fridge for two months.

Saskatoon Berry Sauce

Ingredients

2 Cups fresh Saskatoon berries

1-1/4 Cups water

3/4 Cup sugar, or to taste

2 Tablespoon cornstarch

1 Tablespoon lemon juice

1/2 Teaspoon pure almond extract

Directions

Place the berries and water in a small pot. Bring to a boil. Lower heat so mixture gently simmers. Cook 5 minutes. Whisk the sugar and cornstarch together in a bowl. Stir into berry mixture. Stir in the lemon juice and almond extract. Simmer until sauce is thickened and clear. Serve sauce hot or cold.

Saskatoon Berry Maple Syrup

Ingredients

1 Cup pure maple syrup

1 Cup Saskatoon berries

Directions

Heat maple syrup in a saucepan over medium heat until reduced by half. Add berries. Reduce heat, and simmer until berries are softened, 3 to 5 minutes. Remove from heat. Let steep for 20 minutes.

Ice Creams, Sorbets, Etc.

Saskatoon Berry Buttermilk Ice Cream

Ingredients

2 Cups Saskatoon berries, fresh or frozen

1/3 Cup water

1 Cup heavy cream

1 Vanilla bean, seeds scraped, pod reserved for another use

6 Egg yolks

2/3 Cup granulated sugar

1-1/2 Cups buttermilk

Directions

In a medium saucepan, heat berries and water over medium, stirring with a wooden spoon, muddling the berries. Cook until tender, about 4 minutes for fresh, 6 minutes for frozen. Cool.

Meanwhile, in another medium saucepan over medium, heat cream and vanilla seeds. Bring to a simmer and then remove from heat.

Mix yolks with sugar in a medium bowl. To temper yolks, stirring with a wooden spoon, add a small amount of hot cream mixture into yolk mixture. Pour tempered yolk mixture into the saucepan with remaining hot cream. Return heat to low while stirring continuously with the same wooden spoon. Cook until mixture thickens and coats the back of a spoon, about 5 minutes.

Fold cream mixture in with berries and stir in buttermilk. Allow mixture to cool in the refrigerator, about 1 hour.

Once ice cream base has chilled, prepare ice cream according to manufacturer's instructions. Transfer prepared ice cream to an airtight container and freeze for at least 1 hour before serving, up to two weeks.

‡ Makes 2 servings.

Peach-Berry Frozen Dessert

Ingredients

1 8-Ounce package fat-free cream cheese, softened

2 6-Ounce carton peach fat-free yoghurt with artificial sweetener

1/2 8-Ounce container frozen light whipped dessert topping, thawed

1 Cup chopped, peeled fresh peaches; frozen unsweetened peach slices, thawed, drained, and chopped; or one 8-1/4-ounce can peach slices (juice pack), drained and chopped

1 Cup fresh or frozen unsweetened blueberries, raspberries, and/or strawberries, thawed and drained if frozen

Fresh mint leaves (optional)

Fresh Saskatoon berries (optional)

Directions

In a medium bowl, combine cream cheese and yoghurt. Beat with an electric mixer on medium speed until smooth. Fold in the whipped topping, peaches, and the 1 cup berries.

Pour into a 2-quart square baking dish. Cover with foil and freeze about 8 hours or until firm.

To serve, let stand at room temperature about 45 minutes to thaw slightly. Cut into squares. If desired, garnish with mint leaves and additional berries.

‡ Makes 9 servings.

Saskatoon Frozen Yogurt Pops

Ingredients

1 Cup frozen or fresh Saskatoon berries

3/4 Cup Greek yoghurt

2 to 3 Tablespoons honey

Directions

Puree the ingredients together and pour into your popsicle moulds.

Place in the freezer until they are frozen solid. A little trick to remove them from the moulds easily is to run them under hot water for a few moments to loosen them up.

Saskatoon Ice Cream

Ingredients

2 Cans (14 Ounce/400 Grams each) premium full-fat coconut milk

1 Tablespoon arrowroot starch

1/4 Teaspoon fine sea salt

1 Cup Saskatoon jelly

1/4 Teaspoon pure almond extract

1 Tablespoon fresh lemon juice

1 Cup fresh saskatoon berries (or frozen ones, partially thawed)

Directions

Place the liquid-filled canister from the ice cream machine into the freezer at least 24 hours before planning to churn the ice cream.

In a large saucepan, whisk together one can of the coconut milk, the arrowroot starch, and the salt. Heat over medium-high heat, stirring constantly until bubbles just start to rise to the surface and the mixture thickens. Do not let it come to a full boil.

Remove the saucepan from the heat and whisk in the Saskatoon jelly until it is completely melted. Stir in the remaining can of coconut milk, the almond extract and lemon juice. Whisk until smooth.

Cover and chill for 3 to 4 hours or overnight. Chill the Saskatoon berries, too, if using fresh ones.

Pour the chilled mixture into the ice cream maker, and churn according to manufacturer's directions, about 20 to 30 minutes. About 15 minutes into the churning time, chop the fresh or frozen saskatoon berries, trying to make sure there are no whole berries – this is a little trickier with the frozen ones.

‡ Makes 1-1/2 quarts/litres.

Saskatoon Berry-Lemon Ice

Ingredients

1 Cup water

1/2 Cup sugar

4 Cups fresh Saskatoon berries

1/4 Cup fresh lemon juice

2 Tablespoons finely shredded lemon peel

Directions

In a medium saucepan combine water and sugar; bring to boiling, stirring frequently. Boil gently, uncovered, for 2 minutes. Remove from heat and cool slightly.

In a blender or food processor combine Saskatoon berries, the warm syrup mixture, and lemon juice. Cover and blend or process until almost smooth. Strain mixture through a fine-mesh sieve, discarding seeds. Stir in 1 teaspoon of the lemon peel.

Transfer the mixture to a 3-quart rectangular baking dish or a 13x9x2-inch baking pan. Place in the freezer, uncovered, for 1-1/2 hours or until almost solid.

Remove berry ice from the freezer. Using a fork, break up the ice into a somewhat smooth mixture. Freeze 1 hour more. Break up the ice with a fork and serve in cups. Top each serving with remaining shreds of lemon peel.

‡ Makes 6 to 8 servings.

Jams

Traditional Saskatoon Berry Jam

Ingredients

4 Cups Saskatoons

3 Cups sugar

1/4 Cup water

Juice and grated peel of 1/2 lemon

Directions

Crush Saskatoon berries in a Dutch oven; heat gently until juice starts to flow. Add sugar and water and bring to a boil, stirring constantly. Add lemon juice and peel; bring to a boil and cook, stirring frequently until thick, about 15 minutes.

Pour into hot sterilized jars, leaving 1/4-inch headspace; wipe jar rims thoroughly. Seal and process in a boiling water bath for 10 minutes.

‡ Makes 3 cups.

Saskatoon and Cranberry Jam

Ingredients

2 Cups Saskatoon berries

2 Cups cranberries

3 Cups granulated sugar

1/4 Cup water

Directions

Fill boiling water bath canner with hot water. Place 4 250 mL (1/2 pint) preserving jars in canner over high heat (to sterilize). Place metal snap lids in boiling water. Boil 5 minutes to soften sealing compound. Keep hot until ready to use.

Place fruit in Dutch oven. Crush it a little so the juice will run. Mix in sugar, and water. Allow to stand 15 minutes. Cook until berries are soft, stirring often, mashing them for a more uniform texture, 20 - 30 minutes or until jell stage reached. Remove from heat. Pour into hot sterile jar. Leave 1 cm (1/2 inch) headspace. Clean jar rim. Center metal snap lids. Apply screw band just until fingertip tight. Place in canner. Repeat with remaining jars. Adjust boiling water level to 2.5 cm (1 inch) above jars. Cover canner. Process 5 minutes in boiling water bath. Begin process time when water returns to a boil. Remove from canner. Set upright and spaced apart out of drafts to cool. Cool 24 hours. Test for seal (sealed lids curve downward in the center). Remove screw bands. Wipe jars, label and date. Store in a cool dark location.

‡ Makes 4 250 mL (1/2 pint) jars.

Strawberry-Saskatoon Berry Jam

Ingredients

8 Cups fruit (half Saskatoon berries, half chopped or crushed strawberries)

1 Pouch liquid pectin

5-6 Cups sugar

2 Tablespoons lemon juice

Directions

In a large pot (it will bubble up as it cooks) stir together the fruit, pectin, sugar, and lemon juice. Bring to a full boil and cook, stirring often, for about 20 minutes, or until a small spoonful set on a small dish you've stashed in the fridge or freezer gels enough that your finger leaves a trail when you run it through the puddle of jam.

Ladle into clean, hot jars, wipe rims and seal according to the jar manufacturer's directions (I use the snap lid jars). Set aside to cool. Refrigerate any that won't seal properly.

‡ Makes almost ten 250 mL jars.

Saskatoon and Rhubarb Jam

Ingredients

1 Large navel orange, finely chopped

12 Cups diced rhubarb

6 Cups sugar

7-1/2 Cups Saskatoons

Juice of 1 lemon

Directions

Combine orange, rhubarb, and sugar in a Dutch oven. Bring to boil, stirring constantly. Boil, stirring occasionally, until thick. Add saskatoons and lemon juice. Boil, stirring frequently until thick, about 15 minutes. Pour into hot sterilized jars, leaving 1/4-inch headspace. Wipe jar rims thoroughly. Seal and process in a boiling water bath for 10 minutes.

‡ 16 cups.

Marinades and Rubs

Saskatoon Berry Sauce for Chicken or Pork

Ingredients

2 Cups saskatoon berries (fresh or frozen)

1 Cup water

1/2 Beef bouillon cube

1/2 Teaspoon minced garlic

1 Tablespoon green peppercorn

1/2 Teaspoon thyme

1/2 Teaspoon rosemary

2 Tablespoons cornstarch

1/2 Cup sugar

2 Tablespoons lemon juice

Directions

Place Saskatoon berries in a saucepan with water and bring to a boil. Add bouillon cube, garlic, peppercorns, thyme, and rosemary.

Simmer five minutes. Blend cornstarch and sugar together, add gradually to Saskatoon mixture.

Boil until clear and thick, add lemon juice.

Serve on top of roast or barbequed pork tenderloin or chicken breast.

Saskatoon Chutney

Ingredients

1 Cup Saskatoon berries

2 Green onions, chopped

1-1/2 Teaspoons grated ginger root

1/4 Cup packed brown sugar

1/4 Cup water

2 Tablespoons cider vinegar

1-1/2 Teaspoons cornstarch

Pinch salt

Directions

Combine all ingredients in a large saucepan. Bring to a boil over medium heat; stirring frequently. Cook until the mixture is the consistency of runny jam (about 3-5 minutes). Remove from heat and cool completely.

Meats

Elk with Saskatoon and Port Reduction

Ingredients

Saskatoon Port Reduction

3/4 Tablespoon canola oil

1 Tablespoon fresh ginger, chopped

1 Cup fresh Saskatoon berries

3/4 Cup port

1/3 Cup merlot

1/3 Cup cranberry juice

1 Tablespoon hot sauce

Salt

Pepper

Elk Steak

1-1/2 Tablespoon olive oil

1 Tablespoon rosemary, chopped

1 Tablespoon thyme, chopped

4 (6 Ounce) Top sirloin elk steaks

Salt

Pepper

Directions

<u>Saskatoon Port Reduction</u>

Preheat broiler.

To make the reduction, stir and cook ginger over medium heat with canola oil in a medium pot until ginger starts to release some liquid.

Add the berries to the pot and continue cooking for 2 to 3 minutes.

Stir the port and merlot wine into the berries and ginger and simmer over medium heat until sauce reduces by half, about 15 minutes.

Add the cranberry juice, hot sauce, and bring to a boil; continue boiling for 5 minutes.

Season with salt and pepper, to taste, and keep sauce warm until assembly.

<u>Elk Steak</u>

In a large bowl, stir together olive oil, rosemary, thyme, and salt and pepper, to taste.

Toss steak in the marinade, to cover.

Place steak on a baking sheet and put a baking sheet under the broiler for 4 minutes.

Flip steak, and continue cooking for an additional 4 minutes, until steak is cooked to medium rare.

Saskatoon Pecan Glazed Chicken

Ingredients

4 Bone-in, skin off chicken breasts

Saskatoon Pecan Sauce

1 Tablespoon minced onion

1 Clove garlic, minced

1 Tablespoon butter

1-1/2 Cups Saskatoon berries

1 Tablespoon maple syrup

1 Tablespoon chopped pecans

Salt and pepper to taste

Directions

Preheat barbecue on medium heat.

Grill chicken breasts, bone side down, for about 14 minutes with the lid down. Turn chicken and continue grilling with the lid down until a meat thermometer inserted into the chicken reads 170°F (77°C) (about 10 to 14 minutes). Remove from grill, cover with foil, and let stand for 10 minutes to let the juices settle.

Stir cook onion and garlic in butter for 2 minutes. Add remaining ingredients, bring to a boil, then reduce heat and simmer until sauce is slightly thickened. Spoon sauce over chicken breasts and serve immediately.

Bison Wellington with Saskatoon Berry Shallot Jam

Ingredients

1 Tablespoon butter

1-1/2 Cups thinly sliced shallots

1 Tablespoon apple cider vinegar

1/4 Cup Saskatoon berry or red currant jam

4 (2-inch-thick) Centre-cut bison tenderloin medallions

1 Tablespoon extra-virgin olive oil

Salt and pepper

2 (10-inch) Sheets frozen puff pastry, thawed

1 Egg yolk

Directions

Heat butter in a small pan over medium.

Add shallots and cook until soft and fragrant, about 3 minutes.

Pour in apple cider vinegar and stir. Continue to cook for 1 minute then add jam. Lower heat and simmer until mixture has thickened and is sticky about 5 minutes. Remove from heat and cool in refrigerator.

Pat bison dry with paper towel.

Season bison medallions with salt and pepper on all sides.

Heat olive oil in a large pan over high. Once the pan is heated, sear bison until deep brown on all sides, about 1 minutes per side.

Remove bison from pan and place onto a paper towel-lined plate. Cool in refrigerator.

Preheat oven to 400°F. Line a baking sheet with parchment.

Mix the egg yolk with 2 Tablespoons of water in a small bowl.

Cut each sheet of puff pastry into 4 equal squares. Place 1 bison medallion in the centre of a puff pastry square.

Place 1 heaping spoonful of shallot jam on top of the bison.

Brush egg wash over puff pastry around the bison. Cover with another sheet of puff pastry. You may have to gently stretch the puff pastry over the bison. Seal the puff pastry by pressing a fork around the edges of the pastry. Trim sides with a knife to make straight lines. Brush egg wash over the surface of the pastry.

Repeat with remaining 3 bison medallions and puff pastry. Transfer to a lined baking sheet. Refrigerate for 10 minutes.

Once chilled, bake in centre oven until pastry is golden brown, about 20 minutes. Remove from oven and let rest for 10 minutes before serving.

Venison with Saskatoon Berry Sauce

Ingredients

3 Tablespoons olive oil

2 Tablespoons bacon fat

1/3 Cup sweet onion, finely diced

1 Clove garlic, finely diced

A splash of balsamic vinegar

1 Cup wine

1 Teaspoon sauce (Lingonberry, from Ikea®)

1 Cup Saskatoon berries

1 Tablespoon butter

Venison sausage or tenderloin

Directions

Cook the sausage in a skillet in the oven, when it's just about cooked through, move it on to the stove top and finished off the sausage by searing it on medium-high heat. Then remove the sausage from the pan but keep the drippings and add the oil, bacon fat and onion and garlic. Cook this until the onion is translucent. Once the onion is cooked add the balsamic and wine. Let this reduce, then add the lingonberry sauce and the Saskatoon berries.

Warm the berries through and once the mix is frothing add butter.

Remove from the heat and served with the venison sausage.

‡ Makes 4 servings.

Saskatoon Berry Brined Duck

Ingredients

<u>Brine</u>

2 Gallons of water

2 Cups kosher salt

1 Cup sugar

6 Whole peppercorns

2 Bay leaves, torn into pieces

1-1/2 Cups Saskatoon berries

1/2 White onion, quartered and broken up

1 Whole garlic head, separate cloves and unwrap

2 Ducks

<u>Final</u>

1 Cup butter, melted

Fleur de salt (Kosher salt can be substituted but does not pop with flavour)

Directions

<u>Brine</u>

Combine in a large pot and place 2 ducks. Brine the ducks for 8 to 12 hours.

Drain the brine, pat the ducks dry and place onto pan. Make sure to have something that the ducks can "sit" on so they don't sit on their own juices (cooling rack, vegetables, etc.). Cover with butter (1 cup melted to use over 25 minutes) and place into 500°F oven for 25 minutes. Occasionally baster the ducks with butter.

After the 25 minutes has passed, remove ducks from the oven and lower the heat to 250ºF. Baste the ducks with butter then season with fresh ground pepper and fleur de salt, cover with aluminium foil and place back into the oven for another 25 minutes.

Pork Chops with Saskatoon and Green Apple Chutney

Ingredients

1/2 Cup flour

1 Teaspoon sea salt

1 Teaspoon freshly ground black pepper

4-6 Porkchops (pork loin rib chops are good), 1 to 1-1/2 lbs/450-700gms

1 Tablespoon grapeseed or olive oil

1 Tablespoon butter

<u>Chutney</u>

1 Tablespoon butter

1 Green apple (Granny Smith variety)

1/2 Cup (120ml) red wine

1 Tablespoon Dijon mustard

1/2 Cup Saskatoon jam

1/4 Teaspoon powdered ginger

1/4 Teaspoon ground cardamom

Directions

Mix the flour, salt, and pepper in a heavy-duty Ziploc® plastic bag. Place the pork chops in the bag, seal it and flip and flop them around until they are coated with the flour on all sides.

Preheat a heavy-bottomed skillet over medium heat. Add the oil and butter and heat until the butter sizzles. Add the floured pork chops and sauté them until golden on each side, turning once. The time will depend on the thickness of the chops.

While the pork chops are browning, finely dice the green apple. Heat the butter in a saucepan over medium heat, then add the diced apple and sauté, stirring often, until the apple is translucent about 5 minutes.

Add the red wine, turn the heat to medium-high, and continue cooking and stirring until the wine is reduced and absorbed by the apples. The mixture should have no visible liquid left, but not very dry either. This should take about 5 more minutes.

Stir in the mustard, Saskatoon jam, ginger, and cardamom. Bring to a boil, then reduce heat and simmer chutney for 2 more minutes. Keep warm until the pork chops are cooked.

Serve the pork chops with the chutney and a few wedges of green apple.

‡ Serves 4 to 6.

Pemmican

Ingredients

4 Cups lean meat (deer, beef, caribou, or moose)

3 Cups dried Saskatoon berries

2 Cups rendered fat

Unsalted nuts and about 1 shot of honey

Directions

Meat should be as *lean* as possible and double ground from your butcher if you do not have your own meat grinder. Spread it out very thin on a cookie sheet and dry at 180F for at least 8 hours or until sinewy and crispy. Pound the meat into a near powder consistency using a blender or other tool. Grind the dried fruit, but leave a little bit lumpy for the texture. Heat rendered fat on the stove at medium until liquid. Add liquid fat to dried meat and dried fruit, and mix in nuts and honey. Mix everything by hand. Let cool and store.

‡ Can keep and be consumed for several years.

Pork Tenderloin with Saskatoon Horseradish Glaze

Ingredients

1/2 Cup Chinook "Saskatoon Honey Syrup"

1 Teaspoon chilli powder

1 Tablespoon prepared horseradish

1 Tablespoon olive oil

1 Clove garlic, minced

2 1-Pound pork tenderloins

1 Teaspoon Dijon mustard

1/4 Cup fresh Saskatoon berries

Directions

Combine ingredients, except pork & fresh saskatoons, in a food processor and whirl until smooth. Place pork in a shallow pan and pour half of the glaze over it. Cover and marinate in the refrigerator for 1-2 hrs.

Remove pork from marinade. Heat BBQ to high and quickly sear tenderloins on all sides. This will take 2 to 3 minutes. Turn off one burner, reduce heat to medium, and place pork over the unlit burner to grill with indirect heat until just cooked through and still pink inside (about 30 to 40 minutes) brushing with reserved marinade every 10 minutes to glaze.

Remove pork from grill and let rest, covered, for 5 minutes before slicing into 1-1/2-inch pieces. Reheat remaining marinade to boiling and drizzle a little over pork, then scatter fresh Saskatoons over top.

‡ Serves 4.

Misc. Recipes

Saskatoon and Blue Cheese Dip

Ingredients

1/4 Cup quality balsamic vinegar

1/4 Cup Saskatoon berry jam

2 Tablespoons red wine

1/4 Cup crumbled blue cheese

1 Garlic clove, crushed (optional)

Salt and freshly ground pepper

1/2 Cup olive oil

Directions

Mix all the ingredients except the olive oil in a food processor. Pour in the oil in a steady stream until well combined. Cover and refrigerate, giving it a quick whisk before serving.

Fennel and Saskatoon Berry Stuffing

Ingredients

1 Tablespoon butter

2 Tablespoons olive oil

2 Cups white onion, diced

1-1/2 Cups fennel (anise) bulb, diced

1/2 Teaspoon sea salt

1/2 Teaspoon freshly ground black pepper

1/2 Teaspoon fresh parsley, chopped

10 Cups white and whole wheat bread, cubed (not too fresh)

1/4 Cup shelled pumpkin seeds, toasted, and coarsely chopped

3/4 Cup dried saskatoon berries*

3 Cups chicken stock, homemade or low in sodium

4 Tablespoon pan drippings from roasted turkey

Directions

Grease a large casserole dish with some butter and preheat oven to 350°F (180°C).

Sauté onion and fennel in a pan with remaining butter and oil until lightly brown. Let cool.

Mix all remaining ingredients in a large bowl except drippings.

Place mixture into casserole dish and bake for 1-1/2 hours.

When the turkey is done drizzle pan drippings over stuffing and return to oven at low heat until ready to serve.

Non-Alcohol Drinks

Saskatoon Berry Drink Mix

Ingredients

3 Cups washed saskatoon berries, crushed with a mortar and pestle or a potato masher

1-1/2 Cups water

Simple Syrup

1-1/2 Cups of sugar

3/4 Cups of water

Directions

Place in a large saucepan and heat to boiling. Boil hard for 5 minutes, then remove from heat and cool to room temperature.

Simple Syrup

Mix 1 1/2 cups of sugar and 3/4 cups of water together in a small saucepan and bring to a boil on the stove. Stir constantly to dissolve the sugar. Once the mixture is boiling, remove it from the heat and set aside to cool. (If you want to make your syrup thicker, you can step up the ratio of sugar:water).

Once your ingredients have cooled, run the berries and water through a metal sieve, reserving the liquid. Press the berries into the sieve with the back of a spoon to get all the juice out. You will end up with some berry pulp in the sieve.

Run the saskatoon berry liquid through an even finer sieve if you have one (tightly-woven cheesecloth if you don't). The idea is to make the syrup as clear as possible.

Combine the sugar and the berry juice together and process (if you're canning it) and store in your usual way.

When you want to drink it, just place a few tablespoonsful in a tall glass and add chilled water, diluting the syrup to your taste. This recipe makes about 3 cups of syrup.

Saskatoon Berry Lemonade

Ingredients

8 Cups cold water

2 Cups sugar

3 Cups fresh lemon juice

3 Strips lemon peel

2 Cups Saskatoon berries (or mix with other berries)

Ice cubes

Seltzer or club soda

Directions

Prepare sugar syrup: In 4-quart saucepan, heat 4 cups water with sugar and lemon peel to boiling over high heat, stirring occasionally. Cover saucepan and boil 3 minutes. Remove saucepan from heat.

Meanwhile, in a food processor, pulse berries until pureed. Pour into a medium-mesh sieve set over large bowl and press berry mixture with back of a spoon to remove seeds; discard seeds.

Remove peel from syrup; stir syrup into berry puree with lemon juice and remaining 4 cups water. Makes 13 cups. Pour into large pitcher with tight-fitting lid. Cover and refrigerate until cold, at least 3 hours or up to 2 days. Serve over ice. Add seltzer to taste; garnish with berries and lemon slices.

Other Desserts

Saskatoon Berry Crisp

Ingredients

4 Cups (1 L) freshly picked Saskatoon berries (if using frozen berries, they must be completely thawed, and excess moisture removed)

3/4 Cup flour

1/2 Cup granulated sugar

1/2 Cup packed brown sugar

3/4 Teaspoon cinnamon

1/4 Teaspoon nutmeg

Pinch salt

1/2 Cup cold butter

Directions

Add berries to buttered 10x6-inch baking dish.

In a bowl, mix together flour, granulated sugar, brown sugar, cinnamon, nutmeg, and salt.

Using a pastry blender or two knives, cut in butter until mixture is in coarse crumbs.

Sprinkle flour mixture evenly over berries. Bake at 350°F (180°C) oven for 40 minutes, or until topping is golden brown. Serve warm with whipped cream or ice cream.

Panna Cotta with Saskatoon Berry Sauce

Ingredients

<u>Panna Cotta</u>

2 Cups of half and half (or heavy cream)

2 Cups of 2% or 1% milk

1/2 Cup of white sugar or Splenda®

1 Teaspoon of vanilla (or your favourite liquor)

2 Packets of gelatin

1/2 Cup of cold water

<u>Saskatoon Berry Sauce</u>

2 Cups of fresh or frozen Saskatoon Berries

2 Cups of ginger ale (regular or diet) or 7-Up®

1 Tablespoon of cornstarch

Directions

<u>Panna Cotta</u>

Place the water in a small bowl and sprinkle the gelatin on top. Let stand until you need it in the next step.

In a large saucepan, over medium heat, heat the cream, milk, and sugar until it just starts to boil. Add the gelatin mixture and the vanilla. Stir well until the gelatin is completely dissolved. Remove from heat.

Spoon the mixture into individual serving dishes. Wine glasses make a pretty vessel for this dessert. Can use miniature stemless wine glasses. Put the dishes in the fridge to set for at least 4 hours.

Saskatoon Berry Sauce

Pour the ginger ale into a medium-sized saucepan. Add the cornstarch and mix until it is completely dissolved. Add the Saskatoons. Cook over medium heat until the berries are slightly cooked, and the sauce has thickened – about 15 to 20 minutes. Remove from heat. If you are serving this dish right away let the sauce cool until it is at room temperature, so it doesn't melt the pannacotta. Otherwise, put it in a jar or other container and put it in the fridge until you need it.

When you are ready to serve just spoon the sauce over the pannacotta (as much or as little as you like) and enjoy!

‡ Sauce is good on pancakes or ice cream too.

Saskatoon Cobbler

Ingredients

Filling

3 Cups of Saskatoons

1/2 Cup of sugar

1 Cup of water

1 to 2 Tablespoons lemon juice

2 to 3 Tablespoons cornstarch

Biscuit Topping

1-1/4 Cups of flour
1/4 Cup of cold butter
1/4 Cup of sugar
2 Teaspoons baking powder
Lemon zest from one small lemon
1/2 Teaspoon salt
1/2 Cup of cream

Directions

Filling

Combine the Saskatoons, water and sugar in a large saucepan. Bring to a boil over a medium-high heat. Cook for 10 to 5 minutes until the Saskatoon are the desired softness. Once cooked, spoon into the ramekins in equal amounts.

Biscuit Topping

Measure out all the dry ingredients in a bowl, whisking to ensure they are combined well. Cut in the cold butter until it's crumbled. Add the cream until the dough is moistened and sticks together.

Roll the dough into a log and cut into as many pieces as you need "tops." Flatten the disks and place on top of the sauce in the ramekins. The closer you get to matching the exact size, the less sauce spillage you will get over the side of the ramekins.

If you are using an 8×8 pan, drop the topping by spoonfuls over the filling in the pan.

Bake in a 400°F oven for 15 to 20 minutes, until the biscuits are a golden brown.

Saskatoon Berry Tiramisu Dessert Shooters

Ingredients

1/3 Cup mascarpone

1/2 Cup instant white chocolate pudding

1/2 Cup whipping cream

2 Tablespoons granulated sugar

1 Teaspoon maple extract

4 Ladyfingers (4-6, cut into very small pieces)

3/4 Cup coffee

1 Teaspoon vanilla

1/4 Cup sugar

1-1/2 Cups Saskatoon berries

3-1/2 Tablespoons Kahlua®

1/4 Cup toffee bits

Directions

Break apart ladyfingers a divide between 12 shot glasses (how many you need will depend on the size of your shot glasses and how many you get)

Combine Kahlua® and coffee. Take 2 tablespoons and sprinkle a little of the coffee/Kahlua® mixture over the Ladyfingers in each shot glass, dividing equally between all 12.

<u>Poached Saskatoon Berries</u>

Combine sugar, saskatoon berries, remaining coffee and Kahlua® mixture in a medium saucepan and simmer on the stovetop. Reduce heat, and simmer on medium-low for 5-7 minutes or until tender. Remove berries from pan with a slotted spoon and set aside. Discard Kahlua®/coffee mixture.

Mix mascarpone cheese and white chocolate pudding together in medium-sized bowl.

Beat whipping cream in a separate bowl, then add 2 tablespoons white granulated sugar and maple flavouring when it reaches soft peaks. Beat to stiff peaks.

Layer in shot glass beginning with crushed Ladyfingers, with pudding/cheese mixture, then Saskatoon berries Top with whipped cream and garnish with toffee bits.

Saskatoon Berries with Custard Sauce

Ingredients

1/4 Cup sugar or sugar substitute equivalent to 1/4 cup sugar

2 Tablespoons cornstarch

1/8 Teaspoon salt

1-3/4 Cups fat-free milk

3 Egg yolks, slightly beaten

1 Teaspoon vanilla

4 Cups Saskatoon berries

Directions

<u>Custard</u>

In a heavy medium saucepan, combine sugar (if using), cornstarch, and salt. Stir in milk. Cook and stir over medium heat until thickened and bubbly. Cook and stir for 2 minutes more. Remove from heat.

Gradually whisk about half of the hot mixture into the beaten egg yolks. Return all the egg yolk mixture to the saucepan. Cook and stir over medium heat just until mixture is bubbly. Remove from heat. Quickly cool the custard by placing the saucepan into a bowl half-filled with ice water for 3 minutes, stirring constantly. Strain mixture through a fine-mesh sieve into a medium bowl. Stir in sugar substitute (if using) and vanilla. Cover the surface with plastic wrap. Chill for 2 to 24 hours.

<u>Serve</u>

To serve, divide berries among six dessert dishes. Spoon custard over berries.

‡ Makes 6 servings.

Berry Phyllo Tarts

Ingredients

15 Baked miniature phyllo tart shells (one 2.1-ounce box)

1 6 - 8 Ounce carton low-fat lemon or vanilla yoghurt

2/3 Cup fresh Saskatoon berries (add other fruits if desired)

Directions

Fill phyllo tart shells with yoghurt. Top with blueberries, raspberries, and/or cut-up strawberries. Serve at once or place in a shallow pan; Cover with foil or plastic wrap and chill up to 3 hours before serving. Makes 15 miniature tarts.

Pies

Saskatoon Rhubarb Pie

Ingredients

Filling

4 Cups Saskatoon berries

2 Cups rhubarb (fresh or frozen), chopped

1 Cup granulated sugar

1/4 Cup all-purpose flour (add 1 tablespoon extra flour if using frozen fruit)

Crust

1-1/2 Cups all-purpose flour

1/2 Cup whole-wheat flour

1/2 Teaspoon salt

1/3 Cup butter, chilled

1/3 Cup shortening

1 Small egg

1/2 Teaspoon white vinegar

Cold water

Directions

Filling

1. In a large bowl, combine all the ingredients. Set aside until ready to use.

Crust

Crust: Preheat oven to 350°F.

In a large bowl, combine flours and salt. Using a pastry cutter or two knives, cut in butter until mixture resembles small peas. Add shortening and stir until chunks of shortening are dispersed throughout. Set aside.

In a liquid measuring cup, combine egg and vinegar. Fill a measuring cup with cold water until it reaches the 1/2-cup mark. Whisk to combine. Add the wet ingredients to the dry ingredients and, using a pastry cutter, work as little as possible just to combine. Divide mixture in half and form two equal balls (Don't overwork the pastry.)

On a flour-dusted work surface, roll out one portion of dough into a circle 11 inches in diameter. Roll out remaining dough into a 10-inch circle. Using a sharp knife, cut some artistic air vents in the centre. Pour prepared filling into bottom pie shell. Top with second crust. Trim overhanging dough and crimp edges to seal.

Bake in preheated oven for 10 minutes. Reduce heat to 300°F and bake for another 45 to 60 minutes, until filling is thick and bubbly in the middle and crust is golden brown.

‡ Pie can be frozen after.

Saskatoon Berry Pie

Ingredients

<u>Pastry</u>

5 Cups all-purpose flour

1/4 Cup brown sugar

1 Teaspoon baking powder

1 Teaspoon salt

1 Pound cold lard, cubed

1 Egg, beaten

3/4 cup skim milk

1 Tablespoon vinegar

<u>Filling</u>

4 Cups Saskatoon berries washed and patted dry

1 Tablespoon cornstarch

1 Tablespoon granulated sugar

Directions

<u>Pastry</u>

In a large bowl, whisk together flour, brown sugar, baking powder and salt, breaking up any brown sugar lumps.

Using a pastry blender or two knives, cut lard into flour mixture until it resembles coarse meal, with a few larger pieces remaining.

In a separate bowl, whisk together egg, skim milk and vinegar. Pour egg mixture over flour mixture; stir briskly with a fork until dry ingredients are almost fully incorporated, taking care not to over-mix.

Turn the pastry out onto floured surface; divide into thirds and form into discs. Wrap two discs in plastic wrap and refrigerate or freeze for later use.

Working with remaining third of pastry, divide in half and form into discs. Set one half aside. Place remaining pastry on floured surface and roll to scant 1/4-inch thickness. Carefully transfer to 9-inch pie plate.

Roll reserved pastry disc to scant 1/4-inch thickness and set aside.

Filling

In a large bowl, gently toss berries with cornstarch and granulated sugar. Scrape berries and any juices into pie plate. Using a pastry brush, moisten edge of pastry with 2 teaspoons water.

Top berries with reserved rolled pastry. Trim excess pastry from the edge, leaving an approximately 1-1/2-inch overhang. Turn edge under and crimp as desired to seal. Using a sharp knife, cut vents on top.

Bake pie in 410°F (205°C) for 10 minutes, then reduce heat to 250°F (120°C) and bake for an additional 40 to 50 minutes, or until pastry is golden brown and juices are thickened and bubbling.

Let rest at least 5 minutes before serving.

Saskatoon Pie Fries

Ingredients

<u>Filling</u>

4 Cups Saskatoon berries (fresh or frozen)

1 Tablespoon lemon juice

1 Cup granulated sugar

1/8 Cup cornstarch

1 Tablespoon unsalted butter

<u>Pie Dough</u>

315 Grams all-purpose flour

3/4 teaspoon salt

1 Tablespoon granulated sugar

250 Grams unsalted butter

1/2 Cup ice water

Directions

<u>Filling</u>

Combine all the ingredients except the butter into a heavy bottom sauce pot and place over medium heat.

Once the juices have started to come out of the berries, turn the heat up to high and continue to cook until the liquid has reduced, and the mixture is thick.

Remove from the heat and allow to cool completely before use.

<u>Pie Dough</u>

Dice the butter into 1/4-inch cubes and place into the fridge.

Mix all the dry ingredients together in a stainless-steel mixing bowl.

Add the diced butter to the flour and using a paddle attachment mix at low speed until the butter is peameal size.

Add the ice water and mix until just incorporated.

Wrap the dough and place in the fridge for at least 1 hour.

To assemble, place the filling into a food processor and pulse until the berries have all been broken. Place the mix into a piping bag.

Cut the ball of dough in half.

Roll the dough until 1/4-cm thick and into a rectangular shape (15-inch by 9-inch). Repeat with the second piece.

Starting 1/2-inch from the edge of the pastry, pipe the filling approximately 1-cm thick. Leave a 1-inch space then pipe a second line of the filling. Repeat twice more.

Carefully lay the second sheet over top and gently rest on top. Using a chef's knife, cut in between each row of the filling.

Then cut the strips into 3-inch long pieces and place onto a baking tray lined with parchment paper.

Brush with melted butter and sprinkle with cinnamon sugar. Bake at 350°F for 8 to 10 minutes.

Saskatoon Lemon Pie

Ingredients

<u>Lemon Pie Filling</u>

1 Cup of sugar
1/3 Cup of cornstarch
1/2 Cup of lemon juice
4 Egg yolks
1 Cup of hot water
2 Tablespoons butter

<u>Saskatoon Sauce</u>

3 Cups of Saskatoons
1 Cup of water
2 Tablespoons of cornstarch
1/2 Cup of sugar
1 Teaspoon of almond extract
2 Tablespoons of lemon juice

<u>Pie Shell</u>

2 Cups of flour
3/4 Teaspoon of salt
1 Cup of Crisco®
1 Egg
2 Tablespoon cold water
1 Tablespoon vinegar

Directions

<u>Lemon Pie Filling</u>

In a heavy saucepan, combine 1 cup of sugar and cornstarch; add in lemon juice.

In a small bowl, beat the egg yolks. Whisk into the lemon mixture. Gradually add water and stir constantly.

Cook over medium heat. Bring to a boil and keep stirring while mixture thickens. Remove from heat. Add in butter and stir till fully mixed in.

Saskatoon Sauce

In a large saucepan, combine the saskatoons and the water. Bring to a boil, stirring constantly. Simmer for five minutes to soften the saskatoons. Saskatoons can be mashed with a potato masher.

In a separate bowl, mix cornstarch and sugar together making sure there are no lumps. Slowly add to the Saskatoon mixture, and continue to stir. Cook until thick and sauce is glossy. Add almond extract and lemon juice. Remove from the heat.

Pie Shell

Combine flour, salt, and Crisco® in a large bowl. Use a pastry blender and mash up till Crisco® is pea size.

In a separate smaller bowl, beat the egg, and add in water and vinegar. Pour into the flour mixture and mix with a fork just until combined. This will make two bottom pie shells. You can chill the pie shell pastry in the fridge to allow the Crisco® to firm up a bit.

Preheat over to 375°F.

Sprinkle your rolling surface with flour. Gently roll out half of the pie shell dough, lifting and turning the pastry as you go to make sure it doesn't stick. When ready, line your pie shell. Make sure to crimp your edges to the outer edge of the pie plates so they don't shrink too much when baking.

Bake for 20 minutes, watching carefully, until just slightly brown. Remove from the oven.

Final

Fill while warm. Keep your oven still at 375°F.

Fill your pie shell with the lemon filling. Pop your pies back in the oven for 5 minutes, just to set up the lemon filling.

Remove from the oven. Spread on top with a layer of the Saskatoon sauce. Let cool several hours, or overnight, to fully set up.

Glazed Saskatoon Berry Pie

Ingredients

1 Pie crust

6 Cups Saskatoon berries

1 Cup water

1/4 Cup sugar

2 Tablespoons cornstarch

Red or blue food colouring

Fat-free frozen whipped dessert topping, thawed (optional)

Directions

Prepare pie crust as box instructs. Cool on a wire rack.

Place 1 cup of the Saskatoon berries and the water in a food processor bowl. Cover; process until smooth. Transfer to a small saucepan. Bring to boiling; simmer 2 minutes.

In a medium saucepan stir together sugar and cornstarch; stir in berry mixture. Cook and stir over medium heat until bubbly. Cook and stir for 2 minutes more. Remove from heat; stir in enough red food colouring to tint a rich red colour. Cool to room temperature.

Fold remaining Saskatoons into the cooled mixture; pour into pastry shell. Cover with plastic wrap or foil; chill for 3 to 4 hours. If desired, serve with whipped topping. Makes 8 slices.

‡ Makes 8 servings.

Salads

Fruit Salad

Ingredients

1/2 Fresh pineapple, cleaned and diced into small bites

1 (500 grams) Basket of fresh strawberries, cleaned and halved or quartered, depending on size

1 (500 grams) Basket of fresh Saskatoon berries, cleaned

1 (500 grams) Seedless green grapes, cleaned, stems removed

1 (500 grams) Sweet cherries, pitted and halved (high quality frozen sweet cherries work)

1 (250-400 grams) Basket of blackberries, washed (optional)

1 Granny Smith Apple, cleaned and diced, skin on

1 Red Delicious Apple, cleaned and diced, skin on

Juice of one lemon

3-4 Large bananas, sliced

Juice of another lemon

1/2 Cup granulated sugar

1 (500 grams) Basket of fresh raspberries

Fresh mint

Whipping cream or homemade yoghurt, optional

Directions

Layer each fruit, as listed in above ingredient list, in a large pedestal bowl; ensure the colour of each layer is visible on the outer edge of the bowl, as you continue each layer.

Sprinkle granulated sugar over the entire layer, then add the raspberries on the centre of the bananas. Refrigerate overnight, or for 4 to 6 hours until icy cold and sugar has dissolved. Place in a huge bowl and gently toss. Serve with fresh mint and whipping cream.

‡ Makes 12 to 16 servings.

Saskatoon Berry Chicken Pasta Salad

Ingredients

2-1/2 Cups chicken, cooked, diced

3 Cups penne, rotini, or shells

1 Cup celery, sliced

1 Cup sugar snap peas, in pods

1 Cup Saskatoon berries, fresh

1/2 Cup red peppers, finely chopped

1/4 Cup red onions, chopped

2 to 3 Tablespoons basil, fresh, chopped

Salt, to taste

Pepper, to taste

1/2 Cup olive oil

1/3 Cup red wine vinegar

1/2 Teaspoon salt

1/4 Teaspoon pepper

1/4 Cup parsley, fresh, chopped

1/2 to 3/4 Cup parmesan cheese, grated

Directions

Cook pasta according to package directions.

About one minute before it finishes cooking add the pea pods. Drain and rinse with cold water.

In a large bowl, add pasta, pea pods, chicken, celery, parsley, Saskatoon berries, red pepper, red onion, and basil.

Whisk together olive oil, red wine vinegar, salt, and pepper to make the dressing.

Toss salad with dressing, cover and refrigerate several hours or overnight to blend flavours.

Before serving, toss with the parmesan cheese.

‡ Makes 4 servings.

Saskatoon Spinach Salad

Ingredients

Dressing

1/3 Cup sugar

1/2 Cup Canola oil

1/4 Cup white vinegar

2 Tablespoons Flax seeds, crushed

1-1/2 Teaspoons onions, chopped

1-1/2 Teaspoon Worcestershire sauce

1 Teaspoon poppy seeds

1/2 Teaspoon paprika

Salad

1 Pound (500 grams) spinach, shredded

2 Cups Saskatoon berries, fresh or freshly thawed

1/2 Cup slivered almonds, toasted

Directions

Dressing

Combine ingredients in a tightly covered jar or container and shake well, set aside.

Salad

Combine greens and Saskatoon berries in a large glass bowl. Top with toasted almonds. Add dressing and toss.

‡ Serves 6.

Sauces, Syrups, and Dressings

Saskatoon Berry Sauce

Ingredients

4 Cups of fresh Saskatoons

2 Cups of water

1 Cup of white sugar

4 Tablespoon cornstarch

2 Tablespoon lemon juice

Directions

Combine 1-3/4 cups of water, the sugar, and the Saskatoon berries. Boil for 15-20 minutes, until the juice is very dark and rich with flavour. Some of the berries will start to break down. Saskatoons aren't the most sauce friendly berries, they can be seedy and tough.

Stir the cornstarch into your remaining water add the lemon and then cook 5 minutes more or until the Saskatoons are the texture you want.

‡ Makes 4 cups.

‡ Great on turkey, ice cream and more.

Saskatoon Berry Vinaigrette

Ingredients

3/4 Cup red wine vinegar

3/4 Cup Saskatoon berries

2 Tablespoons honey

1 Cup canola oil

1 Teaspoon fresh thyme, chopped

1/4 Teaspoon salt

1/4 Teaspoon ground black pepper

Directions

Place berries, vinegar and honey in a saucepan. Bring to a boil and then simmer for 4 minutes to soften berries.

Puree with canola oil, thyme, salt, and pepper. Do not crush up all berries, leave some whole for texture. Cool and enjoy. Blueberries can be substituted for Saskatoon berries.

‡ Makes 1 cup.

Soups

Cold Saskatoon Berry Soup

Ingredients

4 cups berries, such as Saskatoons or blueberries

4 cups rhubarb

4 apples

1/2 cup raisins

water, to simmer

Directions

Clean fruit. Chop rhubarb and apples.

Combine four types of fruit in a large pot. Add sufficient water to simmer. Bring to a boil, then simmer 1/2 hour. Cool and serve.

‡ Serves 10 to 15 people.

Warm Saskatoon Berry Soup

Ingredients

1 Cup of dried Saskatoon berries (or fresh)

4 Cups of water

1/2 Cup flour, approx.

Sugar

Cooked or dried meat is optional

Directions

Boil berries in the water until soft.

Slowly stir in flour until it begins to thicken.

Sugar-sweeten to taste.

www.ingramcontent.com/pod-product-compliance
Lightning Source LLC
LaVergne TN
LVHW081324060426
835511LV00011B/1835